DEAR GOD,

WE ARE ALL PERFECT, BEAUTIFUL,
PRECIOUS GEMS.
IF WE REALLY WANT,
WITH YOUR HELP, WE CAN SHINE.

PLEASE HELP ME SHINE FOR YOU
AND FOR EVERYONE!

PLEASE DEAR GOD,

PROTECT MY FAMILY,
BROTHERS AND SISTERS, PARENTS
AND GRANDPARENTS.

PLEASE HELP US
SO THAT WE CARE FOR EACH OTHER
AND BE KIND TO EACH OTHER.

I LOVE MY FAMILY!

DEAR GOD,

PLEASE HELP THE CHILDREN
WHO ARE HURT, FRIGHTENED,
SAD AND ALONE.

MAY THEY FEEL YOUR LOVE!

DEAR HOLY MOTHER,

THANK YOU FOR LOVING, HOLDING
AND PROTECTING ME.

IN YOUR EMBRACE I AM SAFE.

I LOVE YOU VERY MUCH!

DEAR GOD,

I FEEL SO MUCH JOY IN MY
HEART TODAY.

PLEASE HELP ME GIVE THIS GIFT
TO OTHER PEOPLE AND HAVE THEM
FEEL JOY TOO!

I AM SO BLESSED!

DEAR GOD,

PLEASE HELP ME FORGIVE IF
SOMEONE HURTS ME.
BY FORGIVING I SET MY HEART
FREE!

THANK YOU!

DEAR GOD,

YOU ARE MY BEST FRIEND AND
YOU LOVE ME HOW I AM.

I FEEL SAFE WITH YOU AND CAN
TELL YOU ALL MY SECRETS.

THANK YOU FOR BEING MY FRIEND!

DEAR GOD,

THANK YOU FOR HELPING ME
STAY ON YOUR PATH
AND GUIDE ME TO NOT GET LOST
ON MY WAY HOME.

PLEASE KEEP ME SAFE.

PLEASE DEAR ANGELS,

BE WITH ME WHILE I SLEEP
TONIGHT.
WITH YOU I AM PROTECTED AND
SAFE WITH GOD.

GOOD NIGHT, I LOVE YOU...

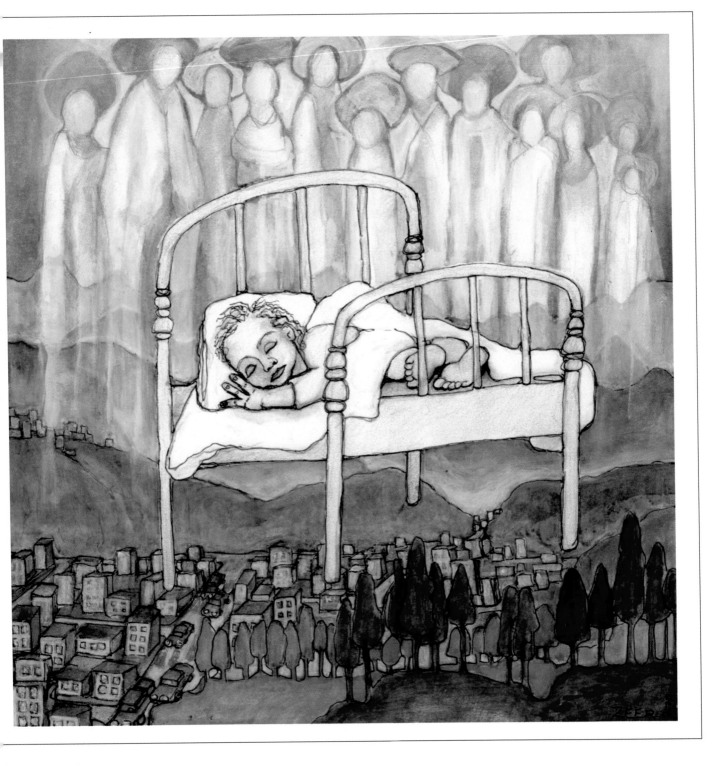

NOW YOU CAN WRITE YOUR OWN PRAYER...

Gabriella Westerbarkey

Rob Zeer

Gabriella and Rob reside in Munich Germany and are friends.

Gabriella was born in Germany and has lived as a spiritual seeker in numerous parts of the world. She is now travelling her serious path Home to God. Rob is from Canada and a renowned exhibiting artist in both Canada and Europe. Gabriella's and Rob's shared spiritual desire has united them with their participation in numerous meditations and seminars together.

Gabriella and Rob believe everyone shares the same longing for God regardless of their religion or perspective that may or may not use the name God. With Gabriella having three grandchildren in Germany and Rob having two grandchildren in Australia, with this book of prayers they hope to introduce God to their grandkids.

This book is an offering of love coming from the realization that prayer resonates with souls of all ages, young or old.

Enjoy!

Made in the USA
Middletown, DE
12 September 2020